GEARED FOR GROWTH BIBLE STUDIES

THE PROBLEMS OF LIFE!

IS THERE AN ANSWER?

BIBLE STUDIES TO IMPACT THE LIVES OF ORDINARY PEOPLE

Written by Ann Edwards

The Word Worldwide

CHRISTIAN
FOCUS

ISBN 1-85792-907-1
ISBN 978-1-85792-907-2

Copyright © WEC International

Published in 2002
and reprinted in 2007
by
Christian Focus Publications,
Geanies House, Fearn,
Ross-shire, IV20 ITW, Scotland, UK
www.christianfocus.com
and
WEC International,
Bulstrode, Oxford Road, Gerrards Cross,
Buckingham-shire, SL9 8SZ, England, UK
www.wec-int.org.uk

Cover design by Alister MacInnes

Printed and bound by Bell & Bain

CONTENTS

QUESTIONS AND NOTES

ANSWER GUIDE

PREFACE
GEARED FOR GROWTH

'Where there's LIFE there's GROWTH:
Where there's GROWTH there's LIFE.'

WHY GROW a study group?

Because as we study the Bible and share together we can

- learn to combat loneliness, depression, staleness, frustration, and other problems
- get to understand and love each other
- become responsive to the Holy Spirit's dealing and obedient to God's Word

and that's GROWTH.

How do you GROW a study group?

- Just start by asking a friend to join you and then aim at expanding your group.
- Study the set portions daily (they are brief and easy: no catches).
- Meet once a week to discuss what you find.
- Befriend others, both Christians and non Christians, and work away together

see how it GROWS!

WHEN you GROW ...

This will happen at school, at home, at work, at play, in your youth group, your student fellowship, women's meetings, mid-week meetings, churches and communities,

you'll be REACHING THROUGH TEACHING

INTRODUCTORY STUDY

FEAR, ANGER, SICKNESS, DEPRESSION, BEREAVEMENT, BROKEN RELATIONSHIPS

We are living in very troubled times. We can see pain and sadness etched on peoples faces as news of another disaster hits the headlines. Tragedy and death brings fear to millions.

September 11th 2001 can never be forgotten. With thousands of lives murdered in such a short space of time while going about their everyday business, anger, hatred and revenge are expressed throughout the nation. Terrorism has left a permanent scar upon New York and affected the lives of millions throughout the world.

The world is full of broken-hearted people. Many of them are disillusioned as they see children living in utter poverty and deprivation. Some parents worry about their teenage children; others experience anger and bitterness because of the circumstances in their lives. People worry about money or the lack of it while others suffer loneliness.

As long as we live in this world we shall meet with difficulties. Problems stem from these and unfortunately not all problems can be avoided. What we need are some answers to help us through the rough times, someone we can turn to who listens with compassion.

God is love, cares about us and longs to help us in all our circumstances. God's problem is that people whom he has created are living without any thought of him. Living on earth without knowledge of him creates problems in people. Because God is holy, he could not look upon sin and had to find a way to save his creation from their rebellious ways. He sent his Son Jesus to die on the cross for us and through Jesus we can be forgiven for all the wrong things we have done. That does not mean all our problems disappear but that he will help us and give us strength to face those difficult times.

In John 16:33 (Amplified Bible), we read, '... In the world you have tribulations, and trials and distresses and frustrations; but be of good cheer, for I have overcome the world'.

Let us consider the following three stories relating to people with real problems and see whether we can help them in their situations. Is there a real answer?

DOMESTIC PROBLEMS

Hilda has become a bitter and resentful woman. As a child she was physically abused and now feels wrongly treated. She has been unable to have any children of her own, is bitter against God for not answering her prayers and jealous of her sister who has four children. Recently she lost her husband after a long and painful illness. She now feels lonely. What steps could you take to help her see God's love?

Discuss how the following Scriptures could be used by God in her situation – Isaiah 54:10; I Samuel 1:4-20; Psalm 34:18,19; 4:8.

Tommy is a young man with no confidence and is worried about the future. At five years of age his mother died and when only ten, his father committed suicide. He was constantly moved from one relative to another. He feels hurt and disappointed at the way life has treated him. He has many unanswered questions. 'Why is life so difficult? Is there anyone who can help me?' How would you answer him?

In Matthew 11:28 Jesus is saying, 'Come to me, all you who are weary and burdened, and I will give you rest.' We know certain scriptures that have helped us but how can we transfer that word into another person's circumstances?

Joe is a married man with three children and feels angry that his wife has left him. He finds life very difficult holding down a job and the responsibility of looking after the children. His eldest son suffers with epilepsy and has learning difficulties. Joe resents his situation and is looking for answers. The anger and stress that he feels have affected his health.

Discuss his situation and what could be done to alleviate his problems? Which of the following scriptures do you think would help him? Psalm 37:3-8; Proverbs 3:5-8.

THE CAUSE OF OUR PROBLEMS

Adam and Eve were created as perfect human beings living in a perfect world. They had fellowship with God and had no problems. In Genesis chapter 3 we read how the serpent (Satan) used his evil influence to tempt Adam and Eve to disobey God. Their disobedience brought a curse upon the earth and all humanity were damaged by this sin right up to this present day. This was the beginning of pain, suffering and hard work.

When we sin, it is a matter of choice. Our problems can be caused by sinful acts that we have done, careless words we have spoken, wrong attitudes that we have, selfishness and greed. However, we can see from the previous illustrations the following:

Hilda was not responsible for the sinful act when she was abused and personal sin did not prevent her from having children; neither was she responsible for her husband's death.

It was not Tommy's sin that was the cause of his mother's death nor was he responsible for the death of his father when he committed suicide.

1. What difference has being a Christian made to the problems you have encountered in your life?

2. What problem areas have you struggled with and how did you overcome them?

STUDY 1

ANGER

QUESTIONS

Unrighteous Anger

DAY 1   *Genesis 4:1-16.*
   a) Why did Cain become angry?

   b) What did God first say to him?

   c) What was the result of his anger?

DAY 2   *1 Samuel 17:26-29; 1 Kings 21:4-14.*
   a) Why did David's brother get angry?

   b) How did David react?

   c) What caused Ahab to be angry?

   d) What other emotions were present?

DAY 3   *1 Samuel 20:27-34.*
   a) Why did Saul become angry?

   b) How did Jonathan feel?

   c) Why did he feel like this?

QUESTIONS (contd.)

Righteous Anger
DAY 4 *Exodus 32:1-14, 19.*
a) Why was God angry?

b) What did Moses ask God?

c) When did Moses get angry?

DAY 5 *Mark 3:1-5; John 2:13-17.*
a) What made Jesus angry?

b) How did Jesus express His anger?

c) How would you explain the anger of Jesus in John's Gospel?

Day 6 *Psalm 37:8; Proverbs 15:1, 18; James 1:19-20*
a) What does the Psalmist say we should do with anger?

b) Write out James 1:20 in your own words.

c) Discuss how you can help angry people.

Day 7 *Ephesians 4:31-32 Romans 12:9; Colossians 3:13*
a) How can we prevent anger leading to sin?

b) Write out three instances in which you became angry.

c) How did you overcome anger?

NOTES

Anger is a powerful emotion often used wrongly to hurt others with words or physical violence. However, anger directed to sin and the mistreatment of others is not wrong. When injustice or sin make you angry, ask God how you can channel that anger and in a constructive way bring about positive change.

Unrighteous Anger

Anger is a dangerous emotion that always threatens to leap out of control and lead to violence, emotional hurt and mental stress. Anger keeps us from developing a spirit that pleases God. Self-control is good but Christ wants us to practice thought control. Killing is a terrible sin but anger is a great sin too if it causes us to violate God's command to love. Cain became angry with his brother Abel and God asked him a question, 'Why are you angry with your brother'? God told him he could master his anger but Cain murdered his brother. King Ahab could not have his own way for he wanted the vineyard belonging to Naboth. When Naboth refused to give it or sell it to him he went away in a rage and later Jezebel had Naboth killed in Ahab's name.

Righteous Anger

While Moses was away from the people they made an idol for themselves. God saw what they had done and became very angry with the people for their idolatry. When Moses descended from the mountain and saw the people dancing around the calf which they had made, his anger burned within him.

Jesus was angry about the Pharisees' uncaring attitude. Jesus expressed his anger by correcting their problem. In Mark 3:1-5 the verses show us how Jesus dealt with the situation that caused him anger when he healed a man on the Sabbath day. Sometimes we can express our anger in unselfish ways. In itself it is not wrong to feel anger, it depends on what we do with it. It is right to be angry about sin and injustice but it is wrong to harbour it and let it smoulder for it will only harm us. Psalm 37:8 tells us to, 'Refrain from anger and turn from wrath; do not fret – it leads only to evil.'

Let us submit our anger to the Lord and ask him to channel it into positive action for good.

STUDY 2

BITTERNESS

QUESTIONS

DAY 1 *Genesis 25:27-34; 27:30-41.*
a) What made Esau bitter?

b) How did he feel towards Jacob?

DAY 2 *Genesis 32:1-11; 33:1-11.*
a) Why was Jacob so fearful in meeting Esau?

b) How did Esau approach Jacob?

DAY 3 *Ruth 1:1-5, 12, 13, 20, 21.*
a) What happened to Naomi when she lived in Moab?

b) How did the bereavements affect her?

c) Discuss how bitterness can affect us?

DAY 4 *Ruth 1:18-22; 2:1, 11, 12, 19-23; 4:13-16.*
a) Who did Naomi say had made life bitter for her?

b) Why do we blame God for our bitterness?

QUESTIONS (contd.)

c) Who helped Naomi to overcome her bitterness?

DAY 5 *1 Samuel 1:1-18.*
a) Why was Hannah unhappy?

b) Who made her life miserable?

c) How did Hannah find her solution?

DAY 6 *Isaiah 38:1-8; Ephesians 4:31-32; Hebrews 12:15.*
a) What was the cause of Hezekiah's bitterness?

b) How did he deal with it?

c) What commands are given regarding bitterness?

DAY 7 *Matthew 6:14-15; Mark 11:25-26; Ephesians 4:32.*
a) What is the result of not forgiving others?

b) How are we to forgive?

c) Has God forgiven you?

NOTES

The dictionary defines 'bitterness' as sharp and disagreeable, harsh, uncomfortable, full of pain. The problem with it is that it never stays the same, it is like a cancer - it grows and pollutes. In the Book of Proverbs 14:10 (Living Bible), we read, 'Only the person involved can know his own bitterness or joy – no one else can really share it.'

Causes of Bitterness

There are many different ways that we can become bitter, usually it is through adverse personal circumstances. In the case of Naomi, it was the loss of her husband and her two sons, yet she was able to overcome by being involved with Ruth. Together they were able to discover God's purposes for their future.

In Hannah's case her problem was in not having a child but she was able to pour out her heart to the Lord, he answered and met her need.

Remedy for Bitterness

First we need to acknowledge the problem. Coming to terms with bitterness seems to be the first step towards getting rid of it. Would you agree? We also need to stop feeding it. We need to learn to recognize it then we have the choice either to embrace it or respond to the grace of God which can free us. If someone has made us feel bitter, we need to learn to forgive.

Peter questioned the Lord as to how often we should forgive. Should it be seven times? No, says Jesus, you should forgive up to seventy times seven.

What is included in forgiveness? Forgetting! It is not easy to forgive and forget but God is able to give us the grace that we need to forgive and leave the memory of the circumstances with God and enjoy his peace. We can use bitter experiences that have taken place in our lives and relationships to become better people.

James 3:13-18 shows us clearly how the Christian person can portray the life of Christ in his good deeds when performed with true humility and wisdom.

STUDY 3

RELATIONSHIPS

QUESTIONS

DAY 1 *Genesis 2:7-9, 15-25.*
a) What kind of relationship did Adam have with God?

b) What need did Adam have that God provided?

DAY 2 *Genesis 3:6-13.*
a) What happened as a result of Adam and Eve's disobedience?

b) Who did Adam blame?

c) How does passing the blame onto another person affect relationships?

DAY 3 *Genesis 16:1-5.*
a) What caused Sarah's problem?

b) How did she try to solve it?

c) Why did Hagar despise Sarah?

DAY 4 *Genesis 16:5-16.*
a) Who did Sarah blame?

b) How did she treat Hagar?

QUESTIONS (contd.)

c) How did Hagar react?

d) What did Hagar learn about God in her struggles?

DAY 5 *Acts 15:36-40; 1 Peter 5:13; 2 Timothy 4:11.*
a) What caused the break in fellowship between Paul and Barnabas?

b) What was the immediate result?

c) How was the problem resolved eventually?

DAY 6 *Matthew 5:23-24; Luke 23:33-34; Matthew 18:13-17.*
a) What is needed in a broken relationship?

b) What help should other Christians give in resolving conflicts between individuals?

c) Discuss problems you might have had in this area of your life?

DAY 7 *1 Samuel 20:1-13, 42.*
a) What are the ingredients of a good relationship?

b) Do you have a good relationship with God?

c) How can it be improved?

NOTES

RELATIONSHIPS

God said it was not good for man to be alone, so he made a helper suitable for him. Adam and Eve had a perfect relationship with each other and with God. After their disobedience, they went and hid from God but God took the initiative to look for them. He called to them and Adam replied, 'I heard you in the garden, and I was afraid because I was naked; and so I hid'. Adam blamed Eve for giving him the fruit of the tree. Eve in turn blamed the serpent. The close fellowship between each other and between them and God was broken. Right relationships with God lead to right relationships with others. Broken relationships can sap our energy, take away our joy and create many problems. It results sometimes in friends not speaking to each other, church members becoming divided, teenagers leaving home in rebellion and anger.

Conflict is normal, it is our reaction to it that affects us. Physical pain motivates us to visit the doctor but emotional pain should motivate us to seek a change of attitude and discover God's remedy for the problem.

Friendship and fellowship are basic needs for every human being. We need each other but there are times when we have a difference of opinion and we no longer enjoy the friendship and relationship that we had. When we bring up the past against others, this reveals a need in our own lives and we need to begin to forgive and forget. God knows we cannot easily forgive and forget but he gives us his grace to help when we make a positive step to forgive others.

Make a list of those with whom you have a problem and by each name write, 'Lord, I forgive'. Now ask God to grant you a forgiving spirit and to drive out any bitterness and fill your heart with his love. Do not wait until you feel like doing it or you never will, so take time and do it now.

Building Relationships

In her book, *Relationships*, Truus Wierda says, 'We can compare the building of relationships with the structure of a bridge.... Good relationships bridge the gap caused by differences in outlook and personality. The piles of the bridge are composed of forgiveness, acceptance, tolerance and spending time together. It is helpful to evaluate our relationships in the light of these principles.'

'Therefore as God's chosen people, holy and dearly loved, clothe yourselves with compassion, kindness, humility, gentleness and patience. Bear with each other, and forgive whatever grievances you may have against one another. Forgive as the Lord forgave you' (Col. 3:12, 13).

STUDY 4

WORRY

QUESTIONS

DAY I *Matthew 6:25-34.*
a) What are some of the things we are told not to worry about?

b) How many times does the word 'worry' occur in these verses? (not in AV)

c) What should be the first priority in our lives?

DAY 2 *Luke 10:38-42.*
a) What was the concern of Martha?

b) Who did she reproach?

c) What did she ask Jesus to do?

d) How did he answer her?

DAY 3 *John 14:1 and 27; Isaiah 26:2-4.*
a) What did Jesus tell his disciples not to do?

b) What did Jesus want to give them instead of worry?

QUESTIONS (contd.)

DAY 4 *Psalm 118:5-9, 13-14; 55:22.*
a) Who should carry our burdens and cares?

b) Discuss the effects of worry.

DAY 5 *Philippians 4:4-7; 1 Peter 5:7.*
a) What are we to be anxious about?

b) How can we overcome worry?

DAY 6 *Matthew 10:29-31; Jeremiah 29:11.*
a) What are we to Jesus?

b) What are the plans of God for us?

DAY 7 *Psalm 107:1-9; Luke 12:22-34.*
a) Who is concerned for us when we are anxious?

b) Why do we get worried?

c) What advice would you give to someone who is deeply worried?

NOTES

What is worry? In some translations of the Bible the word 'worry' is usually translated 'anxiety' or 'care'. The Greek word in the New Testament means to divide, part or tear apart. The word describes the effect of worry and what worry can do to us. Worry is often an anxious concern over the future, something we cannot do anything about and this is why it can tear us apart.

Worry can show us that we have no confidence in the sovereignty of God or in his word and worry can affect us personally. Listen to the words of Jesus in Matthew 6:31, 'So do not worry, saying, "What shall we eat?" or "What shall we drink?" or "What shall we wear?"' And in verse 34, 'Therefore do not worry about tomorrow for tomorrow will worry about itself. Each day has enough trouble of its own.'

Worry is like a rocking chair, you can spend a lot of energy rocking it but it won't get you anywhere. Freedom from anxiety is possible. The answer lies in Scripture where Jesus said simply and directly, 'Stop worrying'. With your mind apply these words of Jesus and say, from this moment on, 'I am going to stop worrying in obedience to the command of Jesus. I am going to release the situation I am worried about to him.' Then, have a time of thanksgiving, which is another antidote to worry. Here is a simple plan you may find useful. Sit down and write out the following.

1. What is my problem?
2. What does God want me to do about it?
3. When, where or how shall I begin?
4. Look for the solution in the Bible.

Many years ago we used to sing a song:

'Said the robin to the sparrow, 'I should really like to know,
Why these anxious human beings rush about and worry so.'
Said the sparrow to the robin, 'Friend I think that it must be,
That they have no Heavenly Father such as cares for you and me.'

In John 14:1 Jesus said to them, 'Do not let your heart be troubled. You believe in and adhere to and trust and rely on God; believe in and adhere to and trust and rely on me' (Amplified Bible).

Jesus has every detail worked out perfectly for each one of us. Just rest on his promises and experience his peace and love in your life.

STUDY 5

TEMPTATION

QUESTIONS

DAY 1 *Genesis 3:1-10.*
a) Who was tempted?

b) What was the result?

c) What were the three aspects of this temptation?

DAY 2 *Genesis 39:1-12; Joshua 7:1-23.*
a) What did Joseph do when faced with temptation?

b) How did Achan react to temptation?

c) Who knew of his sin?

d) What is the difference between temptation and sin?

DAY 3 *James 1:13-15; Luke 4:1-2; 1 Thessalonians 3:5.*
a) Who tempts us?

b) Why does he tempt us?

c) How would you define temptation?

DAY 4 *Matthew 26:40, 41; Ephesians 6:16-18; 1 Peter 5:8-9.*
a) How are we told to react to temptation?

QUESTIONS (contd.)

b) What has God given us to withstand temptation?

c) What does Peter tell us to do?

DAY 5 *Matthew 4:1-11; Hebrews 2:18; 4:15.*
a) How did Jesus deal with temptation?

b) How do we know that he can help us?

c) What does God want us to do when tempted?

DAY 6 *Matthew 6:13; John 8:44; 8:31-36.*
a) Does God lead us into temptation?

b) How did Jesus describe Satan?

c) What did Jesus declare?

DAY 7 *I Corinthians 10:13; 2 Peter 2:9; James 1:2-4.*
a) What promises does God give to us?

b) What blessings can result from temptation?

c) Are you facing temptation now? If you are, why not ask someone in your group or a friend to pray for you to overcome the temptation.

NOTES

Everyone has the tendency within themselves to do evil. The attractiveness of sin is very real. When Eve was first tempted in the Garden of Eden, it came from a thought that led her to doubt God. God had said that they were not to eat of the tree in the middle of the garden or they would die. The serpent planted a seed of doubt into her mind. 'You will not surely die, ... For God knows that when you eat of it your eyes will be opened and you will be like God, knowing good and evil.' When Eve saw that the fruit of the tree was good and pleasing to the eye, she then took the fruit and involved her husband by giving him some of the forbidden fruit.

Temptation often begins by seeing something we want, such as Achan in Joshua 7:20-21. He saw the beautiful robe, two hundred shekels of silver, and a wedge of gold. He coveted them, then he took them. In the Garden of Gethsemane, Jesus told His disciples who were with him to, 'Watch and pray so that you will not fall into temptation. The spirit is willing, but the body is weak' (Matt. 26:41).

They needed to pray for themselves to be prepared for the danger that was coming, but it would have meant so much more for the Lord Jesus if they had watched with him and prayed with him in his great hour of need.

The way to overcome is to watch and pray. Watching means being aware of temptation and being spiritually equipped to fight it. There is nothing wrong in being tempted but it becomes sin when we yield to it (Jas. 1:14-15). Jesus was also tempted in all areas of his life but he never sinned. God has placed at our disposal all that we need to overcome the temptation. Any temptation can be resisted. The first step to victory is to recognize the temptation and then flee from it.

STUDY 6

FEAR

QUESTIONS

DAY 1 *Genesis 3:1-15.*
a) When did fear first enter the world?

b) What was the cause of Adam's fear?

DAY 2 *Exodus 14:10-14.*
a) What caused the children of Israel to fear?

b) How did it affect them?

c) What did Moses advise them to do?

DAY 3 *Psalm 27:1-3; 56:1-4; Mark 4:37-41; Luke 8:50.*
a) What is the opposite to fear?

b) How did the psalmist react to fear?

c) What makes you fearful and how do you handle it?

DAY 4 *1 Samuel 15:24; Proverbs 29:25.*
a) Who did Saul fear? Why?

QUESTIONS (contd.)

b) What does the fear of man do?

c) What is the answer to fear?

DAY 5 *Romans 8:15; 2 Timothy 1:7-12.*
a) What has God not given to us?

b) What has he given?

DAY 6 *Hebrews 13:5-8; Psalm 118:6; 1 John 4:18.*
a) How can the believer have victory over fear?

b) Discuss how love can cast out fear.

DAY 7 *Hebrews 2:14, 15; Matthew 10:28-30; Ecclesiastes 12:13, 14.*
a) Is it natural to fear death and why?

b) Who are we told to fear or be afraid of?

c) Find verses that tell us not to fear or be afraid and memorize them.

NOTES

Fear is an attitude of anxiety or distress. Scripture provides numerous examples of situations in which fear is experienced. Fear can come in many forms. It can strike into the hearts of all. Many are tortured daily. When the children of Israel feared the Egyptians as they marched after them, they cried out to the Lord and complained to Moses, but he was able to assure them, 'Do not be afraid. Stand firm and you will see the deliverance the LORD will bring you today.'

The encouraging words 'fear not' appear in the Bible 366 times, so there is one verse for every day and even one for the leap year as well! The disciples were fearful in the storm on the sea of Galilee, but when Jesus entered the ship their fears went. God said to Abraham in Genesis 15:1, 'Do not be afraid, Abram. I am your shield'. The Lord is our shield to protect us from all our fears. Isaiah reminds us, 'So do not fear, for I am with you; do not be dismayed, for I am your God' (Isa. 41:10).

Any bondage to fear is sin and must be rooted out. God has not given us a spirit of fear. We can overcome fear by:

1. Prayer,
2. Praise,
3. Resisting it and claiming victory through the blood of Jesus,
4. Applying the Word of God.

If your fear persists, be willing to share your fear with a Christian friend, counsellor or leader for extra prayer.

Fear results from keeping things in one's own hands, faith is placing them into God's hands. If we truly love the Lord and have complete confidence in his sovereignty and power we have nothing to fear. All fear can be overcome through the Lord Jesus Christ through his grace and love toward us.

The answer to the problem of inner fearfulness is not solved by our own human efforts to overcome it but in the confident knowledge of God's love for us and his continual control of all our circumstances in life and in death. The more we are filled with his love and allow this amazing fact to fill our minds and hearts, the more we will be able to overcome fear and experience his inner peace.

STUDY 7

BEREAVEMENT

QUESTIONS

DAY 1 *Job 1:1-22, 2:9-10.*
a) Make a list of all that Job lost.

b) What was Job's reaction?

c) How do you think his wife would have felt?

DAY 2 *2 Samuel 18:32, 33; 19:1-10.*
a) Why was David so upset about the death of Absalom?

b) Discuss various ways bereavement can affect us and then how Jesus can help us.

DAY 3 *Matthew 14:1-14.*
a) How did Jesus handle the death of John the Baptist?

b) What does this reveal to us about Jesus?

DAY 4 *John 11.33-38.*
a) Describe the emotions of Martha and Mary.

b) How did this affect Jesus?

QUESTIONS (contd.)

Day 5 *Mark 5:22-24, 35-43.*
a) What was Jairus concerned about?

b) How do you think his servants handled the situation?

c) How did Jesus deal with the situation?

DAY 6 *Luke 7:11-17.*
a) What was so sad about this death?

b) How did Jesus feel?

c) How did Jesus change the situation?

DAY 7 *Luke 24:13-24, 29-36; John 20:19, 20.*
a) How does Luke describe the two on the road to Emmaus?

b) If you had been one of the disciples then, how would you have felt, knowing Jesus had died? How would you have felt meeting him alive?

c) What caused the disciples to be overjoyed?

Do you realize that Jesus died for you and that he can live within your heart?

NOTES

To be bereaved means to be deprived or robbed of a close relative or friend and it causes great heart concern. When we lose someone or something dear to us, then sorrow fills our heart. Job experienced great pain when he lost all that he had: health, possessions cattle and family. So often we blame his wife for her reaction to their situation but how would we react today?

There are many things that contribute to our feeling of loss: children leaving home, moving house, if we lose our health or are made redundant. Any kind of loss will make us feel shattered. People say, 'Time will heal', but often it doesn't and we just learn to live and adjust to our loss.

Jesus himself felt the loss of John the Baptist. When he learnt that John had been beheaded he went to a quiet place by himself. We may feel the need to get alone when we have lost someone close to us.

When the widow of Nain mourned the loss of her son, Jesus was moved with compassion for her. Not only had she lost her only son but she now had no one to care for her. Jesus could identify with her heartache because he was, 'a man of sorrows, and acquainted with grief' (Isa. 53:3, AV). What a comfort it is for the believer that the Saviour feels the pain that we suffer in bereavement and is always there to give help when we need it. God is the God of all comfort. When we come to him, he comforts us in our grief and pain.

The two on the road to Emmaus were sad; they thought they had lost their Master. They appeared to be very disappointed that Jesus had died and were downcast in spirit. As they walked along the road, Jesus drew near to them. As they talked together, Jesus explained the Scriptures to them and their hearts burned within them. They recognized him as they broke bread together and he then disappeared out of their sight. They arose the same hour and returned to Jerusalem to share with the others that Jesus was alive.

John, in his Gospel, writes that the disciples were glad and overjoyed when they knew that Jesus was alive and was able to meet with them again.

We as Christians have the same blessed hope of meeting Jesus one day face to face and also gathering with all those who love him around the banqueting table. Jesus is the resurrection and the life and all believers have received that eternal life in him (John 11:25-26; 1 Cor. 15:20).

What wonderful assurance we have, for Jesus has gone to prepare a place for us and death is not the end but the wonderful beginning of everlasting life.

STUDY 8

DEPRESSION

QUESTIONS

DAY 1 *Psalm 42:1-11.*
a) What questions did the Psalmist ask?

b) What was the answer?

DAY 2 *Psalm 6:1-10.*
a) How was the Psalmist feeling?

b) How was he encouraged?

c) What do you do on difficult days?

DAY 3 *Psalm 25:1-22.*
a) What did David ask God?

b) How was David feeling?

DAY 4 *1 Kings 19:1-18; Matthew 11:28-30.*
a) Why did Elijah run away?

b) What did God give him before spiritual help?

QUESTIONS (contd.)

c) How important is rest for us?

d) What does Jesus tell us to do?

DAY 5 *Job 17:1-16; Psalm 3:1-8.*
a) Describe the feelings of Job?

b) How does Job view the future?

c) What is the hope for the believer?

DAY 6 *Psalm 55:1-8; 32:7.*
a) What did the Psalmist feel like doing?

b) Where is the best place to hide?

c) Share a time when you felt depressed and how you overcame?

DAY 7 *Psalm 34:15-19; Philippians 4:6-7; Lamentations 3:19-26, 32-33.*
a) When we pray about our situations, what should happen?

b) What does God want us to know?

c) Who is God close to?

Depression is a very common experience. Everybody at some time in their lives feels fed up, miserable and sad. The reasons are all different: disappointment, frustration or moods. In some people the depression can be so severe that it rules their lives, in fact, life doesn't seem worth living. Accusing them of self-pity or telling them to pull themselves together does not help them in their situation.

Causes for Depression

Deep depression is an illness and needs treatment. More ordinary depression could be caused by: a reaction to a physical illness, bereavement, stress, overwork, unemployment, problems in a relationship, money worries or side effects from medication. Sometimes talking things over with friends or relatives may see us through. We can get depressed after a stressful event. Circumstances play a part, some women suffer after childbirth.

Life-threatening illnesses can make us feel depressed. Some people seem more vulnerable than others. Some of the symptoms are sorrow, loneliness, despair and feeling forsaken.

Remedy for Depression

You can help yourself – both practically and spiritually. Don't bottle things up, instead have a good cry. Get out and exercise. Eat a good balanced diet. Help someone else in a practical way. Reading God's Word daily is very important. The Psalms cover such a comprehensive collection of emotions and identify perfectly with our human experiences. Pouring out one's heart to the Lord in prayer concerning the problems, frustrations and disappointments will bring peace and healing.

Elijah experienced the depths of discouragement just after his victory on Carmel. It often sets in after great spiritual experiences. God first allowed Elijah to eat, drink and sleep. This is probably what he needed, then after resting and refreshment, God spoke to him and encouraged him to return to his work. Being depressed is not a sign of failure or lack of spirituality.

We must know God personally before we can expect him to give us the help we need. Life is like sailing on the sea, we meet up with storms and we experience some discomfort, but we must always remember that, if we have made Jesus the captain of our ship, he is always on board to help us through the storm and bring us into a safe haven. Let us remember the promise of Jesus in Matthew 11:28, 'Come to me, all you who are weary and burdened, and I will give you rest.'

STUDY 9

DISCOURAGEMENT

QUESTIONS

DAY 1 *Exodus 5:1-9, 22-23; 6:1-12.*
a) What message did Moses give to Israel?

b) What was the cause of their discouragement?

c) How did it affect Moses?

DAY 2 *Numbers 21:1-9.*
a) Why did the people complain?

b) Why did God send the snakes?

c) What did Moses do for them?

DAY 3 *I Samuel 30:1-20.*
a) Why were David and his men distressed?

b) What caused David to get more distressed?

c) How did David face the situation?

DAY 4 *Ezra 4:1-5.*
a) What did the enemies of Judah try to do?

b) Discuss how opposition can discourage us?

QUESTIONS (contd.)

c) Do you know someone who needs encouragement?

d) List ways on how you could bring that encouragement.

DAY 5 *Nehemiah 4:1-20.*
a) By what means did the enemy try to discourage Nehemiah?

b) What did he do?

c) What was the key for him not to give in?

DAY 6 *John 16:17-33.*
a) What did Jesus promise we would experience in the world?

b) How did he encourage his disciples?

c) If we are in Christ, what do we have?

DAY 7 *Acts 4:36; 9:23-30; 11:22-26.*
a) What is the meaning of the name 'Barnabas'?

b) Who did he encourage?

c) What did he do in Antioch?

d) Share how this course has helped you.

NOTES

The children of Israel were very discouraged in Egypt but God saw their situation, heard their groaning and promised that he would bring them out of their bondage but their hearts were closed to the words of deliverance. The Lord gave to Moses and Aaron a supernatural authority which caused Pharaoh and the Israelites to listen to them (Exod. 7:1-2). Some years later after the Lord had delivered them, they grew impatient, complained about God and Moses and the Lord had to deal with them. He allowed snakes to bite them and many people died until they came in repentance to God. Then Moses prayed for the people. How easy it is to complain about God and our spiritual leaders when we are dissatisfied with our lives.

David and his men arrived back at the camp in Ziklag and discovered that it had been raided and burned. The men's wives and children had been taken captive and the men wept until they had no more strength in them. The men started to blame David and were talking of stoning him but David found strength in the Lord. The Bible says he encouraged himself in the Lord his God and asked his advice.

Our great need is to know God and to be filled with the knowledge of his will and to trust in his Word. As we have looked at the problems of life there is an answer in the Word of God. As we triumph over our problems we will be able to help others. In our final study we have looked at discouragement but we see that if we know the Saviour, we serve a God who is able to encourage us through his Word and through his Spirit in our hearts.

The Bible says, 'Praise be to the God and Father of our Lord Jesus Christ, the Father of compassion and the God of all comfort, who comforts us in all our troubles, so that we can comfort those in any trouble, with the comfort we ourselves have received from God' (2 Cor. 1:3, 4).

May each one of us be used by God to bring healing, encouragement and hope to those who are hurting and discouraged, as we meet people on a daily basis.

ANSWER GUIDE

The following pages contain an Answer Guide. It is recommended that answers to the questions be attempted before turning to this guide. It is only a guide and the answers given should not be treated as exhaustive.

GUIDE TO STUDY 1

DAY 1
a) Because the Lord rejected his offering.
b) He asked him why he was angry and told him that if he did what was right, he would be accepted. He also said that sin desired to have him but he had to master it.
c) Murdered his brother. He went away from the Lord's presence (v.16).

DAY 2
a) Maybe jealousy, as Samuel had anointed David to be king.
b) He complained that he couldn't even ask a question!
c) Ahab could not have his own way.
d) Sulking, depression, resentment, disappointment.

DAY 3
a) Because of David's absence. Against his wishes, Saul could not help but notice the care and help Jonathan had given to David. He may have felt that the future ambitions he had for his son could be affected.
b) Full of rage, he didn't eat that day and was very distressed.
c) Because he was grieved at his father's shameful treatment of David.

DAY 4
a) Because of the idolatry of the people.
b) His favour. He wanted God to spare the people. He reminded God of his promises.
c) When he saw the calf and the dancing.

DAY 5
a) The stubborn hearts of the people.
b) He healed the man.
c) It was his reaction to the disrespect for God in the temple – God's house.

DAY 6
a) Refrain or cease from it.
b) Personal.
c) Personal

DAY 7
a) By being kind and compassionate
b) Personal
c) Personal

GUIDE TO STUDY 2

DAY 1 a) He was cheated by his brother Jacob.
b) Bitter and angry.

DAY 2 a) He was fearful because he had a guilty conscience at the way he had treated Esau.
b) He embraced him.

DAY 3 a) Her husband and two sons died.
b) She became bitter and blamed God.
c) Bitterness makes us sharp and disagreeable and can cause us inward pain.

DAY 4 a) God.
b) Personal
c) God, Ruth and Boaz, also many believing women.

DAY 5 a) No children.
b) Peninnah.
c) In prayer as she poured out her soul to God.

DAY 6 a) His illness.
b) He prayed.
c) We are to get rid of it and be kind and compassionate instead.

DAY 7 a) God will not forgive us.
b) As God has forgiven us.
c) Personal.

GUIDE TO STUDY 3

DAY 1
a) Perfect friendship for he walked and talked with God.
b) A companion/helper.

DAY 2
a) Shame and fear entered their lives. Their intimate relationship with God was broken, so they hid from God.
b) Eve.
c) Personal.

DAY 3
a) Sarah had no child.
b) By giving her maid Hagar to Abraham.
c) She might have thought that she was better than Sarah, now that she was pregnant.

DAY 4
a) Abraham.
b) Sarah dealt harshly with her and ill-treated her.
c) She ran away.
d) He is the God who sees every situation, hears our cry and cares.

DAY 5
a) Whether to take John Mark with them, Paul felt that his leaving them earlier had been desertion.
b) Barnabas and Mark went to Cyprus whilst Paul chose Silas as his new fellow-worker.
c) Mark met Peter and worked with him, proving himself. Paul recognized the change in Mark and regarded him as a useful colleague.

DAY 6
a) Love and forgiveness.
b) By recognizing that we have a responsibility towards each other and that real issues need to be dealt with.
c) Personal.

DAY 7
a) Loyalty and kindness and so on.
b) Personal.
c) Spend more time in prayer, read God's Word and enjoy fellowship with other believers.

GUIDE TO STUDY 4

DAY 1
a) What we eat, drink and wear. WE are not to worry about tomorrow.
b) It depends on what version of the Bible you use (six times in the NIV).
c) God and his Kingdom.

DAY 2
a) All the preparations that had to be made.
b) Her sister Mary.
c) To get Mary to help out.
d) He told her to stop worrying about these small things as there was only one thing she really needed to be concerned about.

DAY 3
a) Not to be troubled.
b) His peace. A quiet calm heart, relaxed and trusting.

DAY 4
a) The Lord Jesus Christ.
b) Personal.

DAY 5
a) Nothing.
b) Through prayer and by casting all of our cares upon Jesus.

DAY 6
a) We are of great worth, far more valuable than the sparrows.
b) To prosper us with peace and give us a hope and a future.

DAY 7
a) God
b) Personal.
c) Write out your thoughts here to the question.

GUIDE TO STUDY 5

DAY 1
a) Eve.
b) Both Adam and Eve ate the fruit; they felt shame and guilt.
c) The fact that the fruit was good for food, pleasing to the eye and desirable for gaining wisdom.

DAY 2
a) He refused and ran from it.
b) He saw, he coveted, he took. He yielded to temptation.
c) God.
d) Sin is giving in to temptation.

DAY 3
a) Satan. He often approaches us through our natural appetites, which are not wrong in themselves but can be used in wrong ways.
b) To lead us away from God.
c) Personal. Definition for temptation: enticement to sin, evil and testing of faith. It comes in three stages: desire, sin and death.

DAY 4
a) Watch and pray.
b) Faith, the Word of God and Prayer.
c) To be watchful, firm in our faith, and resist.

DAY 5
a) Through the Word of God.
b) Because Jesus himself experienced and suffered temptation and over came.
c) Pray, resist, recognize temptation and turn away from it.

DAY 6
a) No, but he does allow us to be tested.
b) As the evil one, a liar and a murderer.
c) That if people hold to his teaching the truth would set them free.

DAY 7
a) God will not let us be tempted beyond what we can bear ... he knows how to rescue us.
b) We can mature in the faith if we handle temptation correctly.
c) Personal

GUIDE TO STUDY 6

DAY 1   a) When Adam and Eve sinned against God.
b) His disobedience to God.

DAY 2   a) Egyptians marching after them.
b) They were terrified and they cried out to the Lord.
c) To not be afraid. They were to stand still and see God's deliverance.

DAY 3   a) Faith is the opposite to fear but 'perfect love' casts out all fear.
b) He stated his trust in God.
c) Personal. Encourage each other by sharing individual victories.

DAY 4   a) He feared the people more than God and disobeyed. God did not have the first place in his life.
b) Puts us in a snare.
c) Trust in the Lord.

DAY 5   a) A spirit of timidity or fear.
b) A spirit of sonship, power, love and a calm and well balanced mind.

DAY 6   a) By affirming with confidence that the Lord is our helper; by being filled with God's love.
b) Personal.

DAY 7   a) Because of its finality and the uncertainty of life after death to those who do not believe.
b) God.
c) Personal.

GUIDE TO STUDY 7

DAY 1   a) Animals, servants, children.
b) Job 1:20-22. He fell down and worshipped. He acknowledged that God had acted in his own sovereign way and he praised him.
c) Personal.

DAY 2   a) He was his son and David might have felt partly to blame.
b) Personal.

DAY 3   a) He withdrew to a solitary place probably to grieve the loss of his cousin John.
b) He entered into the experience of human suffering.

DAY 4   a) They were full of grief at the loss of their brother and deeply disappointed because Jesus had not come to them sooner.
b) He was deeply moved and troubled and he wept.

DAY 5   a) The illness of his daughter.
b) Possibly insensitively, as they told him his daughter was dead and not to bother Jesus any more.
c) Jesus ignored what was said about the girl's death and encouraged Jairus to believe.

DAY 6   a) The only son of his widowed mother.
b) He had compassion on this mother.
c) He brought the son back to life and gave him back to his mother causing the people to be filled with awe and praise to God.

DAY 7   a) Downcast.
b) Personal.
c) When they met with the resurrected Christ.

GUIDE TO STUDY 8

DAY 1 a) There are many. He questioned the reason for his sad state and why God had forgotten him.
b) He told his soul to put its hope in God as he would yet praise him.

DAY 2 a) Faint, worn out, anguished and weepy.
b) He knew God was merciful in answering his prayer.
c) Personal. Read God's Word and pray. Listen to music; go for a walk.

DAY 3 a) To not let him be put to shame; to guide him; to not let his enemies triumph over him; to be gracious to him and take away all his sin.
b) Lonely, afflicted, troubled and in distress.

DAY 4 a) Became afraid of Jezebel's threats.
b) Food, water and rest.
c) We need to rest: believers can get so busy in the Lord's work that they overdo things and this can lead to problems.
d) To come to him for rest, when we are weary and burdened.

DAY 5 a) Downcast, grieving and shattered.
b) As without hope.
c) The Lord who can deliver.

DAY 6 a) Escaping from his situation just like a dove could fly away.
b) In Jesus the 'Rock of Ages'.
c) Personal.

DAY 7 a) God will deliver us. God will give us his peace.
b) That he is compassionate and faithful to his promises for his children.
c) To those who are broken-hearted or crushed in spirit.

GUIDE TO STUDY 9

DAY 1
a) The Lord would bring them out of Egypt and set them free.
b) The cruel bondage of Egypt.
c) Because the people refused to listen, Moses was perplexed and very discouraged.

DAY 2
a) They grew impatient because of life in the desert where they had no food or water.
b) To bring them to repentance.
c) He prayed for them.

DAY 3
a) Their camp had been raided and they had lost all their family and possessions.
b) He heard of threats to stone him as he probably was being blamed for what had happened.
c) He encouraged himself in the Lord and found strength.

DAY 4
a) They tried to discourage the people and make them afraid to go on building.
b) Personal.
c) Personal.
d) Personal.

DAY 5
a) By ridicule and threats of death.
b) He watched and prayed and worked.
c) Determination to get on with the work and succeed.

DAY 6
a) Trouble.
b) He reminded them that he had overcome the world (v. 33).
c) Peace.

DAY 7
a) 'Son of Encouragement'. He was an encourager.
b) Paul and a great number of people.
c) He taught and encouraged the believers.
d) Personal.

THE WORD WORLDWIDE

We first heard of WORD WORLDWIDE over twenty years ago when Marie Dinnen, its founder, shared excitedly about the wonderful way ministry to one needy woman had exploded to touch many lives. It was great to see the Word of God being made central in the lives of thousands of men and women, then to witness the life-changing results of them applying the Word to their circumstances. Over the years the vision for WORD WORLDWIDE has not dimmed in the hearts of those who are involved in this ministry. God is still at work through His Word and in today's self-seeking society, the Word is even more relevant to those who desire true meaning and purpose in life. WORD WORLDWIDE is a ministry of WEC International, an interdenominational missionary society, whose sole purpose is to see Christ known, loved and worshipped by all, particularly those who have yet to hear of His wonderful name. This ministry is a vital part of our work and we warmly recommend the WORD WORLDWIDE 'Geared for Growth' Bible studies to you. We know that as you study His Word you will be enriched in your personal walk with Christ. It is our hope that as you are blessed through these studies, you will find opportunities to help others discover a personal relationship with Jesus. As a mission we would encourage you to work with us to make Christ known to the ends of the earth.

Stewart and Jean Moulds – British Directors, **WEC International**.

A full list of over 50 'Geared for Growth' studies can be obtained from:

John and Ann Edwards
5 Louvaine Terrace, Hetton-le-Hole, Tyne & Wear, DH5 9PP
Tel. 0191 5262803 Email: rhysjohn.edwards@virgin.net

UK Website: www.gearedforgrowth.co.uk

OLD TESTAMENT

Triumphs Over Failures: A Study in Judges ISBN 978-1-85792-888-4 (below left)
Messenger of Love: A Study in Malachi ISBN 978-1-85792-885-3
The Beginning of Everything: A Study in Genesis I-II ISBN 0-90806-728-3
Hypocrisy in Religion: A Study in Amos ISBN 0-90806-706-2
Unshakeable Confidence: A Study in Habakkuk & Joel ISBN 0-90806-751-8
A Saviour is Promised: A Study in Isaiah 1 - 39 ISBN 0-90806-755-0
The Throne and Temple: A Study in 1 & 2 Chronicles ISBN 1-85792-910-1
Our Magnificent God: A Study in Isaiah 40 - 66 ISBN 1-85792-909-8
The Cost of Obedience: A Study in Jeremiah ISBN 0-90806-761-5
Focus on Faith: A Study of 10 Old Testament Characters ISBN 1-85792-890-3
Faith, Courage and Perserverance: A Study in Ezra ISBN 1-85792-949-7

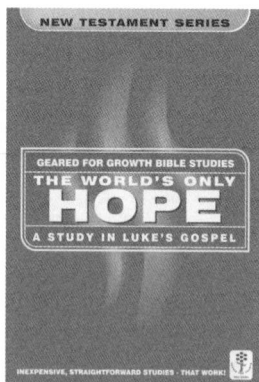

NEW TESTAMENT

The World's Only Hope: A Study in Luke ISBN 1-85792-886-5 (above right)
Walking in Love: A Study in John's Epistles ISBN 1-85792-891-1
Faith that Works: A Study in James ISBN 0-90806-701-1
Made Completely New: A Study in Colossians & Philemon ISBN 0-90806-721-6
Jesus-Christ, Who is He? A Study in John's Gospel ISBN 0-90806-716-X
Entering by Faith: A Study in Hebrews ISBN 1-85792-914-4
Heavenly Living: A Study in Ephesians ISBN 1-85792-911-X
The Early Church: A Study in Acts 1-12 ISBN 0-90806-736-4
The Only Way to be Good: A Study in Romans ISBN 1-85792-950-0
Get Ready: A Study in 1&2 Thessalonians ISBN

CHARACTERS

Abraham: A Study of Genesis 12-25 ISBN 1-85792-887-3 (below left)
Serving the Lord: A Study of Joshua ISBN 1-85792-889-X
Achieving the Impossible: A Study of Nehemiah ISBN 0-90806-707-0
God plans for Good: A Study of Joseph ISBN 0-90806-700-3
A Man After God's Own Heart: A Study of David ISBN 0-90806-746-1
Grace & Grit: A Study of Ruth & Esther ISBN 1-85792-908-X
Men of Courage: A Study of Elijah & Elisha ISBN 1-85792-913-6
Meek but Mighty: A Study of Moses ISBN 1-85792-951-9

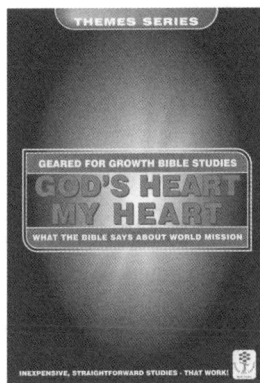

THEMES

God's Heart, My Heart: World Mission ISBN 1-85792-892-X (above right)
Freedom: You Can Find it! ISBN 0-90806-702-X
Freely Forgiven: A Study in Redemption ISBN 0-90806-720-8
The Problems of Life! Is there an Answer? ISBN 1-85792-907-1
Understanding the Way of Salvation ISBN 0-90082-880-3
Saints in Service: 12 Bible Characters ISBN 1-85792-912-8
Finding Christ in the Old Testament: Pre-existence and Prophecy
ISBN 0-90806-739-9

Christian Focus Publications
publishes books for all ages

Our mission statement –

STAYING FAITHFUL
In dependence upon God we seek to help make His infallible word, the Bible, relevant. Our aim is to ensure that the Lord Jesus Christ is presented as the only hope to obtain forgiveness of sin, live a useful life and look forward to heaven with Him.

REACHING OUT
Christ's last command requires us to reach out to our world with His gospel. We seek to help fulfil that by publishing books that point people towards Jesus and help them develop a Christ-like maturity. We aim to equip all levels of readers for life, work, ministry and mission.

Books in our adult range are published in three imprints.

Christian Focus contains popular works including biographies, commentaries, basic doctrine, and Christian living. Our children's books are also published in this imprint.

Mentor focuses on books written at a level suitable for Bible College and seminary students, pastors, and other serious readers; the imprint includes commentaries, doctrinal studies, examination of current issues, and church history.

Christian Heritage contains classic writings from the past.

For details of our titles visit us on our website
www.christianfocus.com